THE 30-MINUTE SHAKESPEARE
LOVE'S LABOR'S LOST

＊

"Nick Newlin's work as a teaching artist for Folger Education during the past thirteen years has provided students, regardless of their experience with Shakespeare or being on stage, a unique opportunity to tread the boards at the Folger Theatre. Working with students to edit Shakespeare's plays for performance at the annual Folger Shakespeare Festivals has enabled students to gain new insights into the Bard's plays, build their skills of comprehension and critical reading, and just plain have fun working collaboratively with their peers.

Folger Education promotes performance-based teaching of Shakespeare's plays, providing students with an interactive approach to Shakespeare's plays in which they participate in a close reading of the text through intellectual, physical, and vocal engagement. Newlin's *The 30-Minute Shakespeare* series is an invaluable resource for teachers of Shakespeare, and for all who are interested in performing the plays."

ROBERT YOUNG, PH.D.
DIRECTOR OF EDUCATION
FOLGER SHAKESPEARE LIBRARY

D1399652

Love's Labor's Lost: The 30-Minute Shakespeare
ISBN 978-1-935550-07-5
Adaptation, essays, and notes © 2010 by Nick Newlin

Cover design by Sarah Juckniess
Printed in the United States of America

Distributed by Consortium Book Sales & Distribution
www.cbsd.com

Nicolo Whimsey Press
www.30MinuteShakespeare.com

Art Director: Sarah Juckniess
Managing Editors: Katherine Little, Leah Gordon

LOVE'S LABOR'S LOST

THE 30-MINUTE SHAKESPEARE

Written by WILLIAM SHAKESPEARE

Abridged AND Edited
by NICK NEWLIN

Nicolo Whimsey
Press

Brandywine, MD

To my sister
Eliza Newlin Carney
for her laughter

Special thanks to Joanne Flynn, Bill Newlin, Eliza Newlin Carney, William and Louisa Newlin, Michael Tolaydo, Hilary Kacser, Sarah Juckniess, Katherine Little, Eva Zimmerman, Leah Gordon, Julie Schaper and all of Consortium, Leo Bowman and the students, faculty, and staff at Banneker Academic High School, and Robert Young Ph.D., and the Folger Shakespeare Library, especially the wonderful Education Department.

✳ TABLE OF CONTENTS

✳ NO EXPERIENCE NECESSARY

I was not a big "actor type" in high school, so if you weren't either, or if the young people you work with are not, then this book is for you. Whether or not you work with "actor types," you can use this book to stage a lively and captivating thirty-minute version of a Shakespeare play. No experience is necessary.

When I was about eleven years old, my parents took me to see Shakespeare's *Two Gentlemen of Verona,* which was being performed as a Broadway musical. I didn't comprehend every word I heard, but I was enthralled with the language, the characters, and the story, and I understood enough of it to follow along. From then on, I associated Shakespeare with *fun.*

Of course Shakespeare is fun. The Elizabethan audiences knew it, which is one reason he was so popular. It didn't matter that some of the language eluded them. The characters were passionate and vibrant, and their conflicts were compelling. Young people study Shakespeare in high school, but more often than not they read his work like a text book and then get quizzed on academic elements of the play, such as plot, theme, and vocabulary. These are all very interesting, but not nearly as interesting as standing up and performing a scene! It is through performance that the play comes alive and all its "academic" elements are revealed. There is nothing more satisfying to a student or teacher than the feeling of "owning" a Shakespeare play, and that can only come from performing it.

But Shakespeare's plays are often two or more hours long, making the performance of an entire play almost out of the question. One can perform a single scene, which is certainly a good start, but what about the story? What about the changes a character goes through as the play progresses? When school groups perform one scene unedited, or when they lump several plays together, the audience can get lost. This is why I have always preferred to tell the story of the play.

The 30-Minute Shakespeare gives students and teachers a chance to get up on their feet and act out a Shakespeare play in half an hour, using his language. The emphasis is on key scenes, with narrative bridges between scenes to keep the audience caught up on the action. The stage directions are built into this script so that young actors do not have to stand in one place; they can move and tell the story with their actions as well as their words. And it can all be done in a classroom during class time!

That is where this book was born: not in a research library, a graduate school lecture, a professional stage, or even an after-school drama club. All of the play cuttings in *The 30-Minute Shakespeare* were first rehearsed in a D.C. public high school English class, and performed successfully at the Folger Shakespeare Library's annual Secondary School Shakespeare Festival. The players were not necessarily "actor types." For many of them, this was their first performance in a play.

Something almost miraculous happens when students perform Shakespeare. They "get" it. By occupying the characters and speaking the words out loud, students gain a level of understanding and appreciation that is unachievable by simply reading the text. That is the magic of a performance-based method of learning Shakespeare, and this book makes the formerly daunting task of staging a Shakespeare play possible for anybody.

With *The 30-Minute Shakespeare* book series I hope to help teachers and students produce a Shakespeare play in a short amount of time, thus jump-starting the process of discovering the beauty, magic, and fun of the Bard. Plot, theme, and language reveal themselves through the performance of these half-hour play cuttings, and everybody involved receives the priceless gift of "owning" a piece of Shakespeare. The result is an experience that is fun and engaging, and one that we can all carry with us as we play out our own lives on the stages of the world.

NICK NEWLIN
Brandywine, MD
March 2010

CHARACTERS IN THE PLAY

The following is a list of characters that appear in this cutting of
Love's Labor's Lost.

Twenty actors performed in the original production. This number can
be increased to about thirty or decreased to about twelve by having
actors share or double roles.

For the full breakdown of characters, see Sample Program.

KING FERDINAND: King of Navarre

BEROWNE

LONGAVILLE } Lords attending on the King

DUMAINE

COSTARD: A clown

BOYET
} Lords attending on the Princess of France
MARCADE

DULL: A constable

THE PRINCESS OF FRANCE

ROSALINE

MARIA } Ladies attending on the Princess

KATHARINE

DON ARMADO: A fantastical Spaniard

SIR NATHANIEL: A curate

HOLOFERNES: A schoolmaster

BOY/MOTH: Page to Don Armado

NARRATORS

✳ SCENE 1. (ACT I, SCENE I)

The King of Navarre's Court.

STAGEHANDS set bench stage right, at an angle, placing table in front of bench; then set throne stage left, at an angle.

Enter NARRATOR from stage rear, coming downstage center.

NARRATOR
> The King of Navarre and his lords vow to retire from the world (especially from women) and study for three years. We will see how long this plan lasts!

Exit NARRATOR stage right.

Enter FERDINAND, BEROWNE, LONGAVILLE, and DUMAINE. FERDINAND stands stage left between the table and bench, placing a scroll and pen on the table. The LORDS stand stage right in front of the table, facing FERDINAND.

FERDINAND
> Let fame, that all hunt after in their lives,
> Live regist'red upon our brazen tombs,
> And then grace us in the disgrace of death;
> You three, Berowne, Dumaine, and Longaville,
> Have sworn for three years' term to live with me,
> My fellow-scholars, and to keep those statutes
> That are recorded in this schedule here:
> Subscribe to your deep oaths, and keep it too.

LONGAVILLE

> I am resolv'd; 'tis but a three years' fast:
> The mind shall banquet, though the body pine.

LONGAVILLE *signs the scroll and crosses stage left.*

DUMAINE

> My loving lord, Dumaine is mortified:
> To love, to wealth, to pomp, I pine and die,
> With all these living in philosophy.

DUMAINE *signs the scroll and moves to* LONGAVILLE'S *right.*

BEROWNE *(walks behind table, looking at scroll)*
> So much, dear liege, I have already sworn,
> That is, to live and study here three years.
> But there are other strict observances:
> As, not to see a woman in that term,
> Which I hope well is not enrolled there:
> And one day in a week to touch no food,
> Which I hope well is not enrolled there.
> O! These are barren tasks, too hard to keep,
> Not to see ladies, study, fast, not sleep.

LONGAVILLE

> You swore to that, Berowne, and to the rest.

BEROWNE

> By yea and nay, sir, then I swore in jest.
> What is the end of study? Let me know.
> Study me how to please the eye indeed,
> By fixing it upon a fairer eye.

LONGAVILLE

> Berowne is like an envious sneaping frost
> That bites the first-born infants of the spring.

BEROWNE *(leaps onto stage right bench, animated)*
Well, say I am: why should proud summer boast
Before the birds have any cause to sing?

FERDINAND
Well, sit out; go home, Berowne; adieu.

FERDINAND *begins to exit stage left, motioning to others to follow.*

BEROWNE *(returns to table)*
No, my good lord; I have sworn to stay with you;
I'll write my name. *(signs his name)*

FERDINAND
How well this yielding rescues thee from shame!

BEROWNE *(reading)*
"Item, That no woman shall come within a mile of
my court."
This article, my liege, yourself must break;
For well you know here comes in embassy
The French king's daughter, with yourself to speak—
A mild of grace and complete majesty—
About surrender up of Aquitaine
To her decrepit, sick, and bedrid father:
Therefore this article is made in vain,
Or vainly comes th' admired princess hither.

FERDINAND
What say you, lords? Why, this was quite forgot.

BEROWNE
So study evermore is over-shot:
We must of force dispense with this decree;
She must lie here on mere necessity.

Necessity will make us all forsworn
Three thousand times within this three years' space.

Enter DULL, *the constable, holding a letter, from stage right.*
He is followed by COSTARD.

LONGAVILLE

Costard the swain shall be our sport;
And so to study three years is but short.

DULL

Signior Arm—Arm—commends you. There's
villainy abroad: this letter will tell you more.
(hands letter to FERDINAND*)*

COSTARD

Sir, the contempts thereof are as touching me.

KING

A letter from the magnificent Armado.

COSTARD

The matter is to me, sir, as concerning Jaquenetta.
The manner of it is, I was taken with the manner.

BEROWNE

In what manner?

COSTARD

In manner and form following, sir; all those three:
I was seen with her in the manor-house, sitting with
her upon the form, and taken following her into
the park; *(sits on bench and pretends to have his arm
around a woman on his right)*—it is the manner of
a man to speak to a woman, for the form,—in some
form.

FERDINAND

Will you hear this letter with attention? *(reading)*
"Great deputy, the welkin's vicegerent and sole
dominator of Navarre, my soul's earth's god and
body's fostering patron."

COSTARD

Not a word of Costard yet.

FERDINAND

Peace!

COSTARD

Be to me, and every man that dares not fight!

FERDINAND

No words!

COSTARD

Of other men's secrets, I beseech you.

FERDINAND

"So it is, besieged with sable-coloured melancholy, I
betook myself to walk, where, I did encounter that
obscene and most preposterous event, there did I
see that low-spirited swain, that base minnow of thy
mirth,"—

COSTARD

Me.

FERDINAND *takes a step downstage to get away from* COSTARD,
but COSTARD *follows, looking over his shoulder.* DULL, *in turn,*
follows COSTARD.

FERDINAND
> "that unlettered small-knowing soul,"—

COSTARD
> Me.

FERDINAND *(takes another step downstage;* COSTARD *follows, then* DULL*)*
> "that shallow vassal,"—

COSTARD
> Still me?

FERDINAND *(he takes yet another step;* COSTARD *follows, then* DULL*)*
> "which, as I remember, hight Costard,"—

COSTARD
> O me!

FERDINAND
> "sorted and consorted, contrary to thy established
> proclaimed edict and continent canon, with—
> with,— *(can't find the word; turns page over)*

COSTARD
> With a wench.

FERDINAND
> "with a child of our grandmother Eve, a female;
> Jaquenetta, which I apprehended with the aforesaid
> swain,— and shall, bring her to trial. Thine, in
> heart-burning heat of duty, DON ADRIANO DE
> ARMADO."

FERDINAND
> But, sirrah, what say you to this?

COSTARD
> Sir, I confess the wench.

FERDINAND
> Did you hear the proclamation?

COSTARD
> I do confess much of the hearing it, but little of the marking of it.

FERDINAND
> Sir, I will pronounce your sentence: you shall fast a week with bran and water.

COSTARD
> I had rather pray a month with mutton and porridge.

FERDINAND
> And Don Armado shall be your keeper.
> My Lord Berowne, see him delivered o'er:
> And go we, lords, to put in practice that
> Which each to other hath so strongly sworn.

Exit FERDINAND, LONGAVILLE, *and* DUMAINE *stage left.*

BEROWNE
> I'll lay my head to any good man's hat
> These oaths and laws will prove an idle scorn.
> Sirrah, come on.

BEROWNE, COSTARD, *and* DULL *begin to exit stage right.*

COSTARD

> I suffer for the truth, sir: for true it is I was taken
> with Jaquenetta, and Jaquenetta is a true girl; and
> therefore welcome the sour cup of prosperity!
> Affliction may one day smile again; and till then, sit
> thee down, sorrow! *(sits on bench)*

BEROWNE *and* DULL *drag bench offstage right, with* COSTARD *remaining seated.*

STAGEHANDS *remove throne and table and set a second bench stage left.*

✳ SCENE 2. (ACT II, SCENE I)

The King of Navarre's Park.

Enter NARRATOR *from stage rear, coming downstage.*

NARRATOR

> The Princess of France and her ladies arrive at
> Navarre. Ferdinand's lords each take an interest in
> one of the Princess's ladies. Maybe that plan not to
> see women was not such a good idea!

Exit NARRATOR *stage right.*

Enter the PRINCESS OF FRANCE, ROSALINE, MARIA, KATHARINE, *and* BOYET *from stage rear.*

BOYET *and the* PRINCESS *stand center, with* BOYET *to the right of the* PRINCESS, *a few feet away from her. The three* LADIES *stand to the left of the* PRINCESS, *in front of stage left bench.*

BOYET

> Now, madam, summon up your dearest spirits:
> Consider who the king your father sends,
> and what's his embassy:
> To parley with Matchless Navarre; the plea of no
> > less weight
> Than Aquitaine, a dowry for a queen.

PRINCESS

> Good Lord Boyet,

You are not ignorant, Navarre hath made a vow,
Till painful study shall outwear three years,
No woman may approach his silent court:
Tell him the daughter of the King of France,
Importunes personal conference with his Grace.

BOYET
Proud of employment, willingly I go.

Exit BOYET *stage right.*

PRINCESS *(calling after him)*
All pride is willing pride, and yours is so.
(to ladies) Who are the votaries,
that are vow-fellows with this virtuous duke?

MARIA *(smiling)*
Lord Longaville is one.

PRINCESS
Know you the man?

MARIA *(steps forward)*
I know him, madam: at a marriage feast, saw I
this Longaville.
A man of sovereign parts, he is esteem'd,
The only soil of his fair virtue's gloss,—
Is a sharp wit match'd with too blunt a will.

PRINCESS
Such short-liv'd wits do wither as they grow.
Who are the rest?

KATHARINE *(steps forward)*
The young Dumaine, a well-accomplish'd youth,

For he hath wit to make an ill shape good,
And shape to win grace though he had no wit.

ROSALINE *(steps forward)*
Another of these students at that time
Was there with him, if I have heard a truth:
Berowne they call him; but a merrier man,
Within the limit of becoming mirth,
I never spent an hour's talk withal.

PRINCESS
God bless my ladies! Are they all in love,
That every one her own hath garnished
With such bedecking ornaments of praise?
Here comes Boyet.

Enter BOYET *from stage right.*

PRINCESS
Now, what admittance, lord?

BOYET *(delighted and excited to be the bearer of good news)*
Navarre had notice of your fair approach,
And he and his competitors in oath
Were all address'd to meet you, gentle lady,
Before I came. Marry, thus much I have learnt;
He rather means to lodge you in the field,
Like one that comes here to besiege his court,
Than seek a dispensation for his oath,
Here comes Navarre.

Enter FERDINAND, LONGAVILLE, DUMAINE, *and* BEROWNE *from stage right. All stand in front of stage right bench.* FERDINAND *takes the* PRINCESS'S *hand and bows graciously.* LONGAVILLE *and* MARIA, KATHARINE *and* DUMAINE, *and* ROSALINE *and* BEROWNE *catch each other's eyes.*

FERDINAND
> Fair Princess, welcome to the court of Navarre.

PRINCESS
> "Fair" I give you back again; and "welcome" I have
> not yet: the roof of this court is too high to be yours,
> and welcome to the wide fields too base to be mine.

FERDINAND
> Hear me, dear lady; I have sworn an oath.

PRINCESS
> I hear your Grace hath sworn out house-keeping:
> 'Tis deadly sin to keep that oath, my lord,
> And sin to break it.

The PRINCESS *turns her back slightly to* FERDINAND, *facing her* LADIES, *who share a small smile/laugh with her. She then gives a paper to* FERDINAND.

FERDINAND *(moving to face the Princess again)*
> Madam, I will, if suddenly I may.

PRINCESS
> You will the sooner that I were away,
> For you'll prove perjur'd if you make me stay.
> *(turns her back again slightly)*

BEROWNE *walks stage left toward* ROSALINE, *clears off the bench with his hat, and motions for her to sit. They both sit on the right side of the bench. All others freeze.*

BEROWNE
> Did not I dance with you in Brabant once?

ROSALINE
> Did not I dance with you in Brabant once?

BEROWNE

I know you did.

ROSALINE

How needless was it then
To ask the question!

BEROWNE

You must not be so quick.

ROSALINE

'Tis long of you, that spur me with such questions.

BEROWNE

Your wit's too hot, it speeds too fast, 'twill tire.

ROSALINE

Not till it leave the rider in the mire.

ROSALINE *stands and moves toward center stage.* BEROWNE, *who has been leaning toward her, falls onto bench. He stands and follows her.*

BEROWNE *(after a slightly uncomfortable silence)*
What time o' day?

ROSALINE

The hour that fools should ask.

BEROWNE

Now fair befall your mask!

ROSALINE

Fair fall the face it covers!

BEROWNE
> And send you many lovers! *(leaning toward her slightly)*

ROSALINE *(turning her back)*
> Amen, so you be none.

ROSALINE walks back to front of bench while BEROWNE stays center stage and gazes forlornly after her.

BEROWNE
> Nay, then will I be gone.

BEROWNE returns to join the other lords stage right. All unfreeze.

FERDINAND
> You may not come, fair Princess, in my gates;
> But here without you shall be so receiv'd
> As you shall deem yourself lodg'd in my heart,
> To-morrow shall we visit you again.

PRINCESS
> Sweet health and fair desires consort your Grace!

FERDINAND *(looking deeply into her eyes)*
> Thy own wish wish I thee in every place.

Exit FERDINAND and his LORDS stage right.

BOYET
> If my observation,—which very seldom lies,
> By the heart's still rhetoric disclosed with eyes,
> Deceive me not now, Navarre is infected.

PRINCESS
> With what?

BOYET
　　With that which we lovers entitle affected.

PRINCESS
　　Your reason.

BOYET *(walking downstage center, painting a picture with his*
　　　　　words and gestures)
　　Why, all his behaviors did make their retire
　　To the court of his eye, peeping thorough desire;
　　His heart, like an agate, with your print impress'd,
　　Proud with his form, in his eye pride express'd;
　　Methought all his senses were lock'd in his eye,
　　As jewels in crystal for some prince to buy.

PRINCESS
　　Come, to our pavilion: Boyet is dispos'd.

BOYET
　　But to speak that in words which his eye hath disclos'd.
　　I only have made a mouth of his eye,
　　By adding a tongue which I know will not lie.

MARIA
　　Thou art an old love-monger, and speak'st skilfully.

Exit ALL *stage rear, led first by the* PRINCESS, *then her* LADIES,
and then BOYET, *winking at the audience.*

✳ **SCENE 3.** (ACT V, SCENE II)

Before the Princess's pavilion.

Enter NARRATOR *from stage rear, coming downstage.*

NARRATOR
> The king and his lords, disguised as Russians, visit
> the ladies, who have their fun by confusing the men.
> Poor misguided men! How will it all end?

Exit NARRATOR *stage right.*

Enter the PRINCESS, KATHARINE, ROSALINE, *and* MARIA *from
stage rear.*

The PRINCESS *and* KATHARINE *stand in front of stage right bench;*
ROSALINE *and* MARIA *stand in front of stage left bench.*

PRINCESS
> Sweet hearts, we shall be rich ere we depart,
> If fairings come thus plentifully in.
> A lady wall'd about with diamonds!
>> *(displays her jewels)*
> Look you what I have from the loving king.
> But, Rosaline, you have a favor too:
> Who sent it? And what is it?

ROSALINE
> I thank Berowne;
> I am compar'd to twenty thousand fairs.

O! He hath drawn my picture in his letter.
(displays a letter and earrings)

PRINCESS

But, Katharine, what was sent to you from fair
Dumaine?

KATHARINE

Madam, this glove.

PRINCESS

Did he not send you twain?

KATHARINE

Yes, madam; and, moreover,
Some thousand verses of a faithful lover;
(displays gloves and a letter)
A huge translation of hypocrisy,
Vilely compil'd, profound simplicity.

MARIA

This, and these pearl, to me sent Longaville;
(displays pearls and a letter)
The letter is too long by half a mile.

PRINCESS

I think no less. Dost thou not wish in heart
The chain were longer and the letter short?

MARIA

Ay, or I would these hands might never part.

PRINCESS

We are wise girls to mock our lovers so.

ROSALINE

They are worse fools to purchase mocking so.
That same Berowne I'll torture ere I go.
O that I knew he were but in by th' week!
How I would make him fawn, and beg, and seek.

PRINCESS

None are so surely caught, when they are catch'd,
As wit turn'd fool: folly, in wisdom hatch'd,
Hath wisdom's warrant and the help of school
And wit's own grace to grace a learned fool.

Enter BOYET *from stage rear.*

PRINCESS

Here comes Boyet, and mirth is in his face. *(stands)*

BOYET

O! I am stabb'd with laughter! Where's her Grace?

PRINCESS

Thy news, Boyet?

BOYET

Prepare, madam, prepare! Love doth approach
disguised,
Armed in arguments; you'll be surpris'd:

PRINCESS

But what, but what, come they to visit us?

BOYET

They do, they do, and are apparell'd thus,
Like Muscovites or Russians, as I guess.
Their purpose is to parley, court, and dance;
And every one his love-feat will advance

Unto his several mistress; which they'll know
By favours several which they did bestow.

PRINCESS

And will they so? The gallants shall be task'd:
For, ladies, we will every one be mask'd;
Hold, Rosaline, this favour thou shalt wear,
        (gives ROSALINE *her jewels)*
And then the king will court thee for his dear;
Hold, take thou this, my sweet, and give me thine,
        *(*ROSALINE *gives the* PRINCESS *her earrings)*
So shall Berowne take me for Rosaline.
And change you favours too; so shall your loves
Woo contrary, deceiv'd by these removes.
        *(*MARIA *gives* KATHARINE *her pearl necklace;*
        KATHARINE *gives* MARIA *her gloves)*

PRINCESS

The effect of my intent is to cross theirs;
They do it but in mocking merriment;
And mock for mock is only my intent.
So shall we stay, mocking intended game,
And they well mock'd, depart away with shame.

SOUND OPERATOR *plays* Sound Cue #1 ("Trumpet sounds").

BOYET

The trumpet sounds: be mask'd; the maskers come.

The LADIES *put their veils over their faces.*

Enter MOTH, FERDINAND, BEROWNE, LONGAVILLE, *and* DUMAINE,
dressed in Russian habits and wearing masks.

MOTH

"All hail, the richest heauties on the earth!"

> *(unsure of which masked lady to talk to)*
> A holy parcel of the fairest dames

The LADIES *turn their backs to him.*

> That ever turn'd their—backs—to mortal views!

BEROWNE
> "Their eyes," villain, "their eyes."

MOTH
> "That ever turn'd their eyes to mortal views!"

BEROWNE
> Is this your perfectness? Be gone, you rogue.

Exit MOTH *stage right.*

ROSALINE *(as* PRINCESS*)*
> What would these strangers? Know their minds, Boyet.

BOYET
> What would you with the princess?

BEROWNE
> Nothing but peace and gentle visitation.

ROSALINE
> What would they, say they?

BOYET
> Nothing but peace and gentle visitation.

ROSALINE
> Why, that they have; and bid them so be gone.

BOYET
> She says you have it, and you may be gone.

FERDINAND
> Say to her we have measur'd many miles
> To tread a measure with her on this grass.

SOUND OPERATOR *plays* Sound Cue # 2 ("Dance music").

FERDINAND *goes to* **ROSALINE**, *who is sitting on downstage side of stage right bench; he offers his hand to dance but she does not return her hand.*

FERDINAND
> Will you not dance? How come you thus estranged?

ROSALINE
> You took the moon at full; but now she's chang'd.

FERDINAND *and* **ROSALINE** *freeze.*

BEROWNE *(goes to the Princess, who is sitting on downstage side of stage left bench)*
> White-handed mistress, one sweet word with thee.

PRINCESS
> Honey, and milk, and sugar; there is three.

BEROWNE *and the* **PRINCESS** *freeze.*

DUMAINE *(goes to* **MARIA**, *who is sitting on upstage side of stage right bench)*
> Will you vouchsafe with me to change a word?

MARIA
> Name it.

DUMAINE
>Fair lady,—

MARIA
>Say you so? Fair lord,
>Take that for your fair lady.

DUMAINE *and* MARIA *freeze.*

LONGAVILLE *goes to* KATHERINE *who is sitting on upstage side of stage left bench.*

KATHARINE
>What, was your visord made without a tongue?

LONGAVILLE
>You have a double tongue within your mask,
>And would afford my speechless visor half.
>One word in private with you ere I die.

KATHARINE
>Bleat softly, then; the butcher hears you cry.

KATHARINE *and* LONGAVILLE *freeze.*

ROSALINE *(unfreezes, along with* FERDINAND*)*
>Not one word more, my maids; break off, break off.

The rest unfreeze.

BEROWNE
>By heaven, all dry-beaten with pure scoff!

FERDINAND
>Farewell, mad wenches; you have simple wits.

PRINCESS
Twenty adieus, my frozen Muscovits.

Exit FERDINAND *and his* LORDS *stage right.*

The LADIES *come to center stage together, laughing.*

ROSALINE
O! They were all in lamentable cases!
The King was weeping-ripe for a good word.

PRINCESS
Berowne did swear himself out of all suit.

MARIA
Dumaine was at my service, and his sword:
"No point" quoth I; my servant straight was mute.

KATHARINE
Lord Longaville said, I came o'er his heart.

BOYET *(from stage right)*
Madam, and pretty mistresses, give ear:
Immediately they will again be here
In their own shapes.

ROSALINE
Good madam, if by me you'll be advis'd,
Let's mock them still, as well known as disguis'd.
Let us complain to them what fools were here,
Disguis'd like Muscovites, in shapeless gear.

BOYET
Ladies, withdraw: the gallants are at hand.

The PRINCESS, ROSALINE, KATHARINE, *and* MARIA *hide behind stage left pillar.*

Enter FERDINAND, BEROWNE, LONGAVILLE, *and* DUMAINE *in their proper habits from stage right.*

FERDINAND

Fair sir, God save you! Where's the princess?

BOYET

Gone to her tent.

The PRINCESS, ROSALINE, MARIA, *and* KATHARINE *come out from behind stage left pillar; the* PRINCESS *greets* FERDINAND *center stage as the other ladies return to their original positions in front of benches.*

FERDINAND

All hail, sweet madam, and fair time of day!

PRINCESS

We have had pastimes here, and pleasant game.
A mess of Russians left us but of late.

FERDINAND

How, madam! Russians?

PRINCESS

Ay, in truth, my lord;
Trim gallants, full of courtship and of state.
(looks at FERDINAND *knowingly)*
Were not you here but even now, disguis'd?

FERDINAND *(confessing)*

Madam, I was.

PRINCESS

Rosaline, what did the Russian whisper in your ear?

ROSALINE

Madam, he swore that he did hold me dear
adding that he would wed me, or else die my lover.

PRINCESS

The noble lord
Most honourably doth uphold his word.

FERDINAND

What mean you, madam? By my life, my troth,
I never swore this lady such an oath.

ROSALINE

By heaven, you did; and, to confirm it plain,
You gave me this: but take it, sir, again.

FERDINAND

My faith and this the princess I did give;
I knew her by this jewel on her sleeve.

PRINCESS

Pardon me, sir, this jewel did she wear;
And Lord Berowne, I thank him, is my dear.

BEROWNE

I see the trick on't: here was a consent,
Knowing aforehand of our merriment,
To dash it like a Christmas comedy.
The ladies did change favors, and then we,
Following the signs, woo'd but the sign of she.
Now, to our perjury to add more terror,
We are again forsworn, in will and error.

Enter COSTARD *from stage rear.*

Welcome, pure wit! Thou part'st a fair fray.

COSTARD
O Lord, sir, they would know
Whether the three Worthies shall come in or no?

BEROWNE
Go, bid them prepare.

Exit COSTARD *stage rear.*

FERDINAND
The ship is under sail, and here she comes amain.

The four men and four women sit as couples on the benches, to watch the show.

Enter COSTARD *from stage rear, to perform "Pompey."*

COSTARD
"I Pompey am"—
That oft in field, with targe and shield, did make
    my foe to sweat:
And travelling along this coast, I here am come
    by chance,
And lay my arms before the legs of this sweet lass
    of France.

BEROWNE
Pompey proves the best Worthy.

Enter SIR NATHANIEL *from stage rear, to perform "Alexander."*

SIR NATHANIEL
"When in the world I liv'd, I was the world's

>   commander;
> By east, west, north, and south, I spread my
>   conquering might:
> My scutcheon plain declares that I am Alisander"—

BEROWNE

> Pompey the Great,—
> Take away the conqueror, take away Alisander.

COSTARD *(to* SIR NATHANIEL*)*

> Run away for shame, Alisander.

Exit SIR NATHANIEL *stage right.*

> But there are Worthies a-coming will speak their
> mind in some other sort.

PRINCESS

> Stand aside, good Pompey.

Enter HOLOFERNES *and* MOTH *from stage rear, to perform "Judas"
and "Hercules," respectively.* MOTH *stands to* HOLOFERNES' *left.*

HOLOFERNES

> "Great Hercules is presented by this imp,
> Whose club kill'd Cerberus, that three-headed canis;
> And when he was a babe, a child, a shrimp,
> Thus did he strangle serpents in his manus.
> Keep some state in thy exit, and vanish.— "

Exit MOTH *stage left.*

HOLOFERNES *stands center stage, declaiming.*

> "Judas I am."—

DUMAINE

> A Judas!

HOLOFERNES

> Not Iscariot, sir.
> "Judas I am, ycliped Maccabaeus."

DUMAINE

> Judas Maccabaeus clipt is plain Judas.

BOYET

> Therefore, as he is an ass, let him go.
> And so adieu, sweet Jude! Nay, why dost thou stay?

DUMAINE

> For the latter end of his name.

BEROWNE

> For the ass to the Jude? Give it him:—Jud-as, away!

HOLOFERNES

> This is not generous, not gentle, not humble.

Exit HOLOFERNES *stage right.*

PRINCESS

> Alas! Poor Maccabaeus, how hath he been baited.

Enter ARMADO, *coming stage right to perform "Hector."*

BEROWNE

> Hide thy head, Achilles: here comes Hector in arms.

ARMADO

> "The armipotent Mars, of lances the almighty,
> Gave Hector a gift, the heir of Ilion;

A man so breath'd that certain he would fight ye,
From morn till night, out of his pavilion.
I am that flower," —

DUMAINE

That mint.

LONGAVILLE

That columbine.

ARMADO

Sweet Lord Longaville, rein thy tongue.
I will forward with my device. *(draws his sword
     toward* COSTARD, *who is stage left)*
By the north pole, I do challenge thee.

COSTARD

I'll slash; I'll do it by the sword.
I bepray you, let me borrow my arms again.

DUMAINE

Room for the incensed Worthies!

COSTARD

I'll do it in my shirt.

DUMAINE

Most resolute Pompey hath made the challenge!

ARMADO

Sweet bloods, I both may and will.

ARMADO *and* COSTARD *are about to fight, and* MOTH *is trying to
separate them.*

Enter MONSIEUR MARCADE, *a messenger, from stage rear.*

MARCADE
God save you, madam!

PRINCESS
Welcome, Marcade;
But that thou interrupt'st our merriment.

MARCADE
I am sorry, madam; for the news I bring
Is heavy in my tongue. The king your father—

PRINCESS
Dead, for my life!

MARCADE
Even so: my tale is told.

BEROWNE
Worthies away! The scene begins to cloud.

First MOTH, *then* COSTARD, *then* ARMADO *exit, but* ARMADO *turns before exiting.*

ARMADO
For mine own part, I breathe free breath.

Exit ARMADO.

FERDINAND *(bowing his head, wishing to comfort the* PRINCESS
but not feeling bold enough)
How fares your Majesty?

PRINCESS *(in mourning)*
Boyet, prepare: I will away to-night.

FERDINAND
Madam, not so: I do beseech you stay.

PRINCESS
Farewell, worthy lord!
A heavy heart bears not a nimble tongue.

BEROWNE *(stepping forward)*
Honest plain words best pierce the ear of grief;
For your fair sakes have we play'd foul play with
    our oaths.
Your beauty, ladies,
Hath much deform'd us, fashioning our humours
Even to the opposed end of our intents;

PRINCESS
We have receiv'd your letters, full of love;
Your favours, the ambassadors of love;
And, in our maiden council, rated them
At courtship, pleasant jest, and courtesy,
and therefore met your loves
In their own fashion, like a merriment.

DUMAINE
Our letters, madam, show'd much more than jest.

LONGAVILLE
So did our looks.

ROSALINE
We did not quote them so.

FERDINAND
Now, at the latest minute of the hour,
Grant us your loves.

PRINCESS *(to* FERDINAND*)*
>A time, methinks, too short
>To make a world-without-end bargain in.
>No, no, my lord, your Grace is perjur'd much,
>Full of dear guiltiness; and therefore this:
>Go with speed
>To some forlorn and naked hermitage,
>Remote from all the pleasures of the world;
>There stay until the twelve celestial signs
>Have brought about the annual reckoning.
>Then, at the expiration of the year,
>Come, challenge me, challenge me by these deserts;
>And, by this virgin palm now kissing thine,
>I will be thine;

FERDINAND
>Hence hermit, then. My heart is in thy breast.

DUMAINE *(to* KATHARINE*)*
>But what to me, my love? But what to me?

KATHARINE
>Come when the King doth to my lady come;
>Then, if I have much love, I'll give you some.

DUMAINE
>I'll serve thee true and faithfully till then.

KATHARINE
>Yet swear not, lest ye be forsworn again.

LONGAVILLE *(to* MARIA*)*
>What says Maria?

MARIA

> At the twelvemonth's end
> I'll change my black gown for a faithful friend.

LONGAVILLE

> I'll stay with patience; but the time is long.

BEROWNE *(to* ROSALINE*)*

> Mistress, look on me;
> Impose some service on me for thy love.

ROSALINE

> My lord Berowne,
> You shall this twelvemonth term, from day to day,
> Visit the speechless sick, and still converse
> With groaning wretches; and your task shall be,
> With all the fierce endeavour of your wit
> To enforce the pained impotent to smile.
> A jest's prosperity lies in the ear
> Of him that hears it, never in the tongue
> Of him that makes it:

BEROWNE

> A twelvemonth! Well, befall what will befall,
> I'll jest a twelvemonth in an hospital.

PRINCESS *(to the* FERDINAND*)*

> Ay, sweet my lord; and so I take my leave.

FERDINAND

> No, madam; we will bring you on your way.

The PRINCESS *shakes her head no.*

BEROWNE

> Our wooing doth not end like an old play:

Jack hath not Jill; these ladies' courtesy
Might well have made our sport a comedy.

FERDINAND
Come, sir, it wants a twelvemonth and a day,
And then 'twill end.

BEROWNE
That's too long for a play.

Enter ARMADO *from stage rear.*

ARMADO
Sweet Majesty, vouchsafe me,—will you hear the
dialogue that the two learned men have compiled
in praise of the owl and the cuckoo? It should have
followed in the end of our show.

FERDINAND
Call them forth quickly; we will do so.

ARMADO
Holla! Approach.

Enter HOLOFERNES, NATHANIEL, MOTH, COSTARD, *and others from
stage rear.*

This is Hiems, Winter; maintained by the owl,
Ver, begin.

ALL *(standing in a line with a simple right/left step and reciting
together)*
When all aloud the wind doth blow,
And coughing drowns the parson's saw,
And birds sit brooding in the snow,
And Marian's nose looks red and raw,

When roasted crabs hiss in the bowl,
Then nightly sings the staring owl:
Tu-who;
Tu-whit, to-who—a merry note,
While greasy Joan doth keel the pot.

ARMADO

The words of Mercury are harsh after the songs
    of Apollo.
(to audience) You that way: *(gestures to self and cast)*
    we this way.

All hold hands and take a bow. Exeunt.

✳ PERFORMING SHAKESPEARE

HOW *THE 30-MINUTE SHAKESPEARE* WAS BORN

In 1981 I performed a "Shakespeare Juggling" piece called "To Juggle or Not To Juggle" at the first Folger Library Secondary School Shakespeare Festival. The audience consisted of about 200 Washington, D.C. area high school students who had just performed thirty-minute versions of Shakespeare plays for each other and were jubilant over the experience. I was dressed in a jester's outfit, and my job was to entertain them. I juggled and jested and played with Shakespeare's words, notably Hamlet's "To be or not to be" soliloquy, to very enthusiastic response. I was struck by how much my "Shakespeare Juggling" resonated with a group who had just performed Shakespeare themselves. "Getting" Shakespeare is a heady feeling, especially for adolescents, and I am continually delighted at how much joy and satisfaction young people derive from performing Shakespeare. Simply reading and studying this great playwright does not even come close to inspiring the kind of enthusiasm that comes from performance.

Surprisingly, many of these students were not "actor types." A good percentage of the students performing Shakespeare that day were part of an English class which had rehearsed the plays during class time. Fifteen years later, when I first started directing plays in D.C. public schools as a Teaching Artist with the Folger Shakespeare Library, I entered a ninth grade English class as a guest and spent two or three days a week for two or three months preparing students for the Folger's annual Secondary School Shakespeare Festival. I have conducted this annual residency with the Folger ever since. Every year for seven action-packed days, eight groups of students between grades seven and twelve tread the boards onstage at the Folger's Elizabethan Theatre, a grand recreation of a sixteenth-century venue with a three-tiered gallery, carved oak columns, and a sky-painted canopy.

As noted on the Folger website (www.folger.edu), "The festival is a celebration of the Bard, not a competition. Festival commentators—drawn from the professional theater and Shakespeare education communities—recognize exceptional performances, student directors, and good spirit amongst the students with selected awards at the end of each day. They are also available to share feedback with the students."

My annual Folger Teaching Artist engagement, directing a Shakespeare play in a public high school English class, is the most challenging and the most rewarding thing I do all year. I hope this book can bring you the same rewards.

GETTING STARTED

GAMES

How can you get an English class (or any other group of young people, or even adults) to start the seemingly daunting task of performing a Shakespeare play? You have already successfully completed the critical first step, which is buying this book. You hold in your hand a performance-ready, thirty-minute cutting of a Shakespeare play, with stage directions to get the actors moving about the stage purposefully. But it's a good idea to warm the group up with some theater games.

One good initial exercise is called "Positive/Negative Salutations." Students stand in two lines facing each other (four or five students in each line) and, reading from index cards, greet each other, first with a "Positive" salutation in Shakespeare's language (using actual phrases from the plays), followed by a "negative" greeting.

Additionally, short vocal exercises are an essential part of the preparation process. The following is a very simple and effective vocal warm-up: Beginning with the number two, have the whole group count to twenty using increments of two (i.e., "Two, four, six . . ."). Increase the volume slightly with each number, reaching top volume with "twenty," and then decrease the volume while counting back down, so that the students are practically whispering when they arrive again at "two." This exercise teaches dynamics and allows them to get loud as a group without any individual pressure. Frequently during a rehearsal period, if a student is mumbling inaudibly, I will refer back to this exercise as a reminder that we can and often do belt it out!

"Stomping Words" is a game that is very helpful at getting a handle on Shakespeare's rhythm. Choose a passage in iambic pentameter and have the group members walk around the room in a circle, stomping their feet on the second beat of each line:

Two **house**-holds, **both** a-**like** in **dig**-nity
In **fair** Ve-**ro**na **Where** we **lay** our **scene**

Do the same thing with a prose passage, and have the students discuss their experience with it, including points at which there is an extra beat, etc., and what, if anything, it might signify.

I end every vocal warm-up with a group reading of one of the speeches from the play, emphasizing diction and projection, bouncing off consonants, and encouraging the group members to listen to each other so that they can speak the lines together in unison. For variety I will throw in some classic "tongue twisters" too, such as, "The sixth sheik's sixth sheep is sick."

The Folger Shakespeare Library's website (http://www.folger.edu) and their book series *Shakespeare Set Free*, edited by Peggy O'Brien, are two great resources for getting started with a performance-based teaching of Shakespeare in the classroom. The Folger website has numerous helpful resources and activities, many submitted by teachers, for helping a class actively participate in the process of getting to know a Shakespeare play. For more simple theater games, Viola Spolin's *Theatre Games for the Classroom* is very helpful, as is one I use frequently, *Theatre Games for Young Performers.*

HATS AND PROPS

Introducing a few hats and props early in the process is a good way to get the action going. Hats, in particular, provide a nice avenue for giving young actors a non-verbal way of getting into character. In the opening weeks, when students are still holding onto their scripts, a hat can give an actor a way to "feel" like a character. Young actors are natural masters at injecting their own personality into what they wear, and even small choices made with how a hat is worn (jauntily, shadily, cockily, mysteriously) provide a starting point for discussion of specific characters, their traits, and their relationships with other characters. All such discussions always lead back to one thing: the text. "Mining the text" is consistently the best strategy for uncovering the mystery of Shakespeare's language. That is where all the answers lie: in the words themselves.

WHAT DO THE WORDS MEAN?

It is essential that young actors know what they are saying when they recite Shakespeare. If not, they might as well be scat singing, riffing on sounds and rhythm but not conveying a specific meaning. The real question is: What do the words mean? The answer is multifaceted, and can be found in more than one place. The New Folger Library paperback editions of the plays themselves (edited by Barbara Mowat and Paul Werstine, Washington Square Press) are a great resource for understanding Shakespeare's words and passages and "translating" them into modern English. These editions also contain chapters on Shakespeare's language, his life, his theater, a "Modern Perspective," and further reading. There is a wealth of scholarship embedded in these wonderful books, and I make it a point to read them cover to cover before embarking on a play-directing project. At the very least, it is a good idea for any adult who intends to direct a Shakespeare play with a group of students to go through the explanatory notes that appear on the pages facing the text. These explanatory notes are an indispensable "translation tool."

The best way to get students to understand what Shakespeare's words mean is to ask them what they think they mean. Students have their own associations with the words and with how they sound and feel. The best ideas on how to perform Shakespeare often come directly from the students, not from anybody else's notion. If a student has an idea or feeling about a word or passage, and it resonates with her emotionally, physically, or spiritually, then Shakespeare's words can be a vehicle for her feelings. That can result in some powerful performances!

I make it my job as director to read the explanatory notes in the Folger text, but I make it clear to the students that almost "anything goes" when trying to understand Shakespeare. There are no wrong interpretations. Students have their own experiences, with some shared and some uniquely their own. If someone has an association with the phrase "canker-blossom," or if the words make that student or his character feel or act a certain way, then that is the "right" way to decipher it.

I encourage the students to refer to the Folger text's explanatory notes and to keep a pocket dictionary handy. Young actors must attach some meaning to every word or line they recite. If I feel an actor is glossing over a word, I will stop him and ask him what he is saying. If he doesn't know, we will figure it out together as a group.

PROCESS VS. PRODUCT

The process of learning Shakespeare by performing one of his plays is more important than whether everybody remembers his lines or whether somebody misses a cue or an entrance. But my Teaching Artist residencies have always had the end goal of a public performance for about 200 other students, so naturally the performance starts to take precedence over the process somewhere around dress rehearsal in the students' minds. It is my job to make sure the actors are prepared— otherwise they will remember the embarrassing moment of a public mistake and not the glorious triumph of owning a Shakespeare play. In one of my earlier years of play directing, I was sitting in the audience as one of my narrators stood frozen on stage for at least a minute, trying to remember her opening line. I started scrambling in my backpack below my seat for a script, at last prompting her from the audience. Despite her fine performance, that embarrassing moment is all she remembered from the whole experience. Since then I have made sure to assign at least one person to prompt from backstage if necessary. Additionally, I inform the entire cast that if somebody is dying alone out there, it is okay to rescue him or her with an offstage prompt.

There is always a certain amount of stage fright that will accompany a performance, especially a public one for an unfamiliar audience. As a director, I live with stage fright as well, even though I am not appearing on stage. The only antidote to this is work and preparation. If a young actor is struggling with her lines, I make sure to arrange for a session where we run lines over the telephone. I try to set up a buddy system so that students can run lines with their peers, and this often works well. But if somebody does not have a "buddy," I will personally make the time to help out myself. As I assure my students from the outset, I am not going to let them fail or embarrass themselves. They need an experienced leader. And if the leader has experience in teaching but not in directing Shakespeare, then he needs this book!

It is a good idea to culminate in a public performance, as opposed to an in-class project, even if it is only for another classroom. Student actors want to show their newfound Shakespearian thespian skills to an outside group, and this goal motivates them to do a good job. In that respect, "product" is important. Another wonderful bonus to performing a play is that it is a unifying group effort. Students learn teamwork. They learn to give focus to another actor when he is speaking, and to play off of other characters. I like to end each performance with the entire cast reciting a passage in unison. This is a powerful ending, one that reaffirms the unity of the group.

SEEING SHAKESPEARE PERFORMED

It is very helpful for young actors to see Shakespeare performed by a group of professionals, whether they are appearing live on stage (preferable but not always possible) or on film. Because an entire play can take up two or more full class periods, time may be an issue. I am fortunate because thanks to a local foundation that underwrites theater education in the schools, I have been able to take my school groups to a Folger Theatre matinee of the play that they are performing. I always pick a play that is being performed locally that season. But not all group leaders are that lucky. Fortunately, there is the Internet, specifically YouTube. A quick YouTube search for "Shakespeare" can unearth thousands of results, many appropriate for the classroom.

The first "Hamlet" result showed an 18-year-old African-American actor on the streets of Camden, New Jersey, delivering a riveting performance of Hamlet's "The play's the thing." The second clip was from *Cat Head Theatre,* an animation of cats performing Hamlet. Of course, YouTube boasts not just alley cats and feline thespians, but also clips by true legends of the stage, such as John Gielgud and Richard Burton. These clips can be saved and shown in classrooms, providing useful inspiration.

One advantage of the amazing variety of clips available on YouTube is that students can witness the wide range of interpretations for any given scene, speech, or character in Shakespeare, thus freeing them from any preconceived notion that there is a "right" way to do it. Furthermore, modern interpretations of the Bard may appeal to those who are put off by the "thees and thous" of Elizabethan speech.

By seeing Shakespeare performed either live or on film, students are able to hear the cadence, rhythm, vocal dynamics, and pronunciation of the language, and they can appreciate the life that other actors breathe into the characters. They get to see the story told dramatically, which inspires them to tell their own version.

PUTTING IT ALL TOGETHER

THE STEPS

After a few sessions of theater games to warm up the group, it's time to begin the process of casting the play. Each play cutting in *The 30-Minute Shakespeare* series includes a cast list and a sample program, demonstrating which parts have been divided. Cast size is generally between twelve and thirty students, with major roles frequently assigned to more than one performer. In other words, one student may play Juliet in the first scene, another in the second scene, and yet another in the third. This will distribute the parts evenly so that there is no "star of the show." Furthermore, this prevents actors from being burdened with too many lines. If I have an actor who is particularly talented or enthusiastic, I will give her a bigger role. It is important to go with the grain—one cast member's enthusiasm can be contagious.

I provide the performer of each shared role with a similar head-piece and/or cape, so that the audience can keep track of the characters. When there are sets of twins, I try to use blue shirts and red shirts, so that the audience has at least a fighting chance of figuring it out! Other than these costume consistencies, I rely on the text and the audience's observance to sort out the doubling of characters. Generally, the audience can follow because we are telling the story.

Some participants are shy and do not wish to speak at all on stage. To these students I assign non-speaking parts and technical roles such as sound operator and stage manager. However, I always get everybody on stage at some point, even if it is just for the final group speech, because I want every group member to experience what it is like to be on a stage as part of an ensemble.

CASTING THE PLAY

Young people can be self-conscious and nervous with "formal" auditions, especially if they have little or no acting experience.

I conduct what I call an "informal" audition process. I hand out a questionnaire asking students if there is any particular role that they desire, whether they play a musical instrument. To get a feel for them as people, I also ask them to list one or two hobbies or interests. Occasionally this will inform my casting decisions. If someone can juggle, and the play has the part of a Fool, that skill may come in handy. Dancing or martial arts abilities can also be applied to roles.

For the auditions, I do not use the cut script. I have students stand and read from the Folger edition of the complete text in order to hear how they fare with the longer passages. I encourage them to breathe and carry their vocal energy all the way to the end of a long line of text. I also urge them to play with diction, projection, modulation, and dynamics, elements of speech that we have worked on in our vocal warm-ups and theater games.

I base my casting choices largely on reading ability, vocal strength, and enthusiasm for the project. If someone has requested a particular role, I try to honor that request. I explain that even with a small part, an actor can create a vivid character that adds a lot to the play. Wide variations in personality types can be utilized: if there are two students cast as Romeo, one brooding and one effusive, I try to put the more brooding Romeo in an early lovelorn scene, and place the effusive Romeo in the balcony scene. Occasionally one gets lucky, and the doubling of characters provides a way to match personality types with different aspects of a character's personality. But also be aware of the potential serendipity of non-traditional casting. For example, I have had one of the smallest students in the class play a powerful Othello. True power comes from within!

Generally, I have more females than males in a class, so women are more likely (and more willing) to play male characters than vice versa.

Rare is the high school boy who is brave enough to play a female character, which is unfortunate because it can reap hilarious results.

GET OUTSIDE HELP

Every time there is a fight scene in one of the plays I am directing, I call on my friend Michael Tolaydo, a professional actor and theater professor at St. Mary's College, who is an expert in all aspects of theater, including fight choreography. Not only does Michael stage the fight, but he does so in a way that furthers the action of the play, highlighting character's traits and bringing out the best in the student actors. Fight choreography must be done by an expert or somebody could get hurt. In the absence of such help, super slow-motion fights are always a safe bet and can be quite effective, especially when accompanied by a soundtrack on the boom box.

During dress rehearsals I invite my friend Hilary Kacser. a Washington-area actor and dialect coach for two decades. Because I bring her in late in the rehearsal process, I have her direct her comments to me, which I then filter and relay to the cast. This avoids confusing the cast with a second set of directions. This caveat only applies to general directorial comments from outside visitors. Comments on specific artistic disciplines such as dance, music, and stage combat can come from the outside experts themselves.

If you work in a school, you might have helpful resources within your own building, such as a music or dance teacher who could contribute their expertise to a scene. If nobody is available in your school, try seeking out a member of the local professional theater. Many local performing artists will be glad to help, and the students are usually thrilled to have a visit from a professional performer.

LET STUDENTS BRING THEMSELVES INTO THE PLAY

The best ideas often come from the students themselves. If a young actor has a notion of how to play a scene, I will always give that idea a try. In a rehearsal of *Henry IV, Part 1,* one traveler jumped into the other's arms when they were robbed. It got a huge laugh. This was something that they did on instinct. We kept that bit for the performance, and it worked wonderfully.

As a director, you have to foster an environment in which that kind of spontaneity can occur. The students have to feel safe to experiment. In the same production of *Henry IV*, Falstaff and Hal invented a little fist bump "secret handshake" to use in the battle scene. The students were having fun and bringing parts of themselves into the play. Shakespeare himself would have approved. When possible I try to err on the side of fun because if the young actors are having fun, then they will commit themselves to the project. The beauty of the language, the story, the characters, and the pathos will follow.

There is a balance to be achieved here, however. In that same production of *Henry IV, Part 1*, the student who played Bardolph was having a great time with her character. She carried a leather wineskin around and offered it up to the other characters in the tavern. It was a prop with which she developed a comic relationship. At the end of our thirty-minute *Henry IV, Part 1*, I added a scene from *Henry IV, Part 2* as a coda: The new King Henry V (formerly Falstaff's drinking and carousing buddy Hal) rejects Falstaff, banishing him from within ten miles of the King. It is a sad and sobering moment, one of the most powerful in the play.

But at the performance, in the middle of the King's rejection speech (played by a female student, and her only speech), Bardolph offered her flask to King Henry and got a big laugh, thus not only upstaging the King but also undermining the seriousness and poignancy of the whole scene. She did not know any better; she was bringing herself to the character as I had been encouraging her to do. But it was inappropriate, and in subsequent seasons, if I foresaw something like that happening as an individual joyfully occupied a character, I attempted to prevent it. Some things we cannot predict. Now I make sure to issue a statement warning against changing any of the blocking on show day, and to watch out for upstaging one's peers.

FOUR FORMS OF ENGAGEMENT: VOCAL, EMOTIONAL, PHYSICAL, AND INTELLECTUAL

When directing a Shakespeare play with a group of students, I always start with the words themselves because the words have the power to engage the emotions, mind, and body. Also, I start with the words in action, as in the previously mentioned exercise, "Positive and Negative Salutations." Students become physically engaged; their bodies react to the images the words evoke. The words have the power to trigger a switch in both the teller and the listener, eliciting both an emotional and physical reaction. I have never heard a student utter the line "Fie! Fie! You counterfeit, you puppet you!" without seeing him change before my eyes. His spine stiffens, his eyes widen, and his fingers point menacingly.

Having used Shakespeare's words to engage the students emotionally and physically, one can then return to the text for a more reflective discussion of what the words mean to us personally. I always make sure to leave at least a few class periods open for discussion of the text, line by line, to ensure that students understand intellectually what they feel viscerally. The advantage to a performance-based teaching of Shakespeare is that by engaging students vocally, emotionally, and physically, it is then much easier to engage them intellectually because they are invested in the words, the characters, and the story. We always start on our feet, and later we sit and talk.

SIX ELEMENTS OF DRAMA: PLOT, CHARACTER, THEME, DICTION, MUSIC, AND SPECTACLE

Over two thousand years ago, Aristotle's *Poetics* outlined six elements of drama, in order of importance: Plot, Character, Theme, Diction, Music, and Spectacle. Because Shakespeare was foremost a playwright, it is helpful to take a brief look at these six elements as they relate to directing a Shakespeare play in the classroom.

PLOT (ACTION)

To Aristotle, plot was the most important element. One of the purposes of *The 30-Minute Shakespeare* is to provide a script that tells Shakespeare's stories, as opposed to concentrating on one scene. In a thirty-minute edit of a Shakespeare play, some plot elements are necessarily omitted. For the sake of a full understanding of the characters' relationships and motivations, it is helpful to make short plot summaries of each scene so that students are aware of their characters' arcs throughout the play. The scene descriptions in the Folger editions are sufficient to fill in the plot holes. Students can read the descriptions aloud during class time to ensure that the story is clear and that no plot elements are neglected. Additionally, there are one-page charts in the Folger editions of *Shakespeare Set Free,* indicating characters' relations graphically, with lines connecting families and factions to give students a visual representation of what can often be complex interrelationships, particularly in Shakespeare's history plays.

Young actors love action. That is why *The 30-Minute Shakespeare* includes dynamic blocking (stage direction) that allows students to tell the story in a physically dramatic fashion. Characters' movements on the stage are always motivated by the text itself.

CHARACTER

I consider myself a facilitator and a director more than an acting teacher. I want the students' understanding of their characters to spring from the text and the story. From there, I encourage them to consider how their character might talk, walk, stand, sit, eat, and drink. I also urge students to consider characters' motivations, objectives, and relationships, and I will ask pointed questions to that end during the rehearsal process. I try not to show the students how I would perform a scene, but if no ideas are forthcoming from anybody in the class, I will suggest a minimum of two possibilities for how the character might respond.

At times students may want more guidance and examples. Over thirteen years of directing plays in the classroom, I have wavered between wanting all the ideas to come from the students, and deciding that I need to be more of a "director," telling them what I would like to see them doing. It is a fine line, but in recent years I have decided that if I don't see enough dynamic action or characterization, I will step in and "direct" more. But I always make sure to leave room for students to bring themselves into the characters because their own ideas are invariably the best.

THEME (THOUGHTS, IDEAS)

In a typical English classroom, theme will be a big topic for discussion of a Shakespeare play. Using a performance-based method of teaching Shakespeare, an understanding of the play's themes develops from "mining the text" and exploring Shakespeare's words and his story. If the students understand what they are saying and how that relates to their characters and the overall story, the plays' themes will emerge clearly. We always return to the text itself. There are a number of elegant computer programs, such as www.wordle.net, that will count the number of recurring words in a passage and illustrate them graphically. For example, if the word "jealousy" comes up more than any other word in Othello, it will appear in a larger font. Seeing the words displayed by size in this way can offer up illuminating insights into the interaction between words in the text and the play's themes. Your computer-minded students might enjoy searching for such tidbits. There are more internet tools and websites in the Additional Resources section at the back of this book.

I cannot overstress the importance of acting out the play in understanding its themes. By embodying the roles of Othello and Iago and reciting their words, students do not simply comprehend the themes intellectually, but understand them kinesthetically, physically, and emotionally. They are essentially *living* the characters' jealousy, pride, and feelings about race. The themes of appearance vs.

reality, good vs. evil, honesty, misrepresentation, and self-knowledge (or lack thereof) become physically felt as well as intellectually understood. Performing Shakespeare delivers a richer understanding than that which comes from just reading the play. Students can now relate the characters' conflicts to their own struggles.

DICTION (LANGUAGE)

If I had to cite one thing I would like my actors to take from their experience of performing a play by William Shakespeare, it is an appreciation and understanding of the beauty of Shakespeare's language. The language is where it all begins and ends. Shakespeare's stories are dramatic, his characters are rich and complex, and his settings are exotic and fascinating, but it is through his language that these all achieve their richness. This leads me to spend more time on language than on any other element of the performance.

Starting with daily vocal warm-ups, many of them using parts of the script or other Shakespearean passages, I consistently emphasize the importance of the words. Young actors often lack experience in speaking clearly and projecting their voices outward, so in addition to comprehension, I emphasize projection, diction, breathing, pacing, dynamics, coloring of words, and vocal energy. *Theatre Games for Young Performers* contains many effective vocal exercises, as does the Folger's *Shakespeare Set Free* series. Consistent emphasis on all aspects of Shakespeare's language, especially on how to speak it effectively, is the most important element to any Shakespeare performance with a young cast.

MUSIC

A little music can go a long way in setting a mood for a thirty-minute Shakespeare play. I usually open the show with a short passage of music to set the tone. Thirty seconds of music played on a boom box operated by a student can provide a nice introduction to the play, create an atmosphere for the audience, and give the actors a sense of place and feeling.

iTunes is a good starting point for choosing your music. Typing in "Shakespeare" or "Hamlet" or "jealousy" (if you are going for a theme) will result in an excellent selection of aural performance enhancers at the very reasonable price of ninety-nine cents each (or free of charge, see Additional Resources section). Likewise, fight sounds, foreboding sounds, weather sounds (rain, thunder), trumpet sounds, etc. are all readily available online at affordable cost. I typically include three sound cues in a play, just enough to enhance but not overpower a production. The boom box operator sits on the far right or left of the stage, not backstage, so he can see the action. This also has the added benefit of having somebody out there with a script, capable of prompting in a pinch.

SPECTACLE

Aristotle considered spectacle the least important aspect of drama. Students tend to be surprised at this since we are used to being bombarded with production values on TV and video, often at the expense of substance. In my early days of putting on student productions, I would find myself hamstrung by my own ambitions in the realm of scenic design.

A simple bench or two chairs set on the stage are sufficient. The sense of "place" can be achieved through language and acting. Simple set dressing, a few key props, and some tasteful, emblematic costume pieces will go a long way toward providing all the "spectacle" you need.

In the stage directions to the plays in *The 30-Minute Shakespeare* series, I make frequent use of two large pillars stage left and right at the Folger Shakespeare Library's Elizabethan Theatre. I also have characters frequently entering and exiting from "stage rear." Your stage will have a different layout. Take a good look at the performing space you will be using and see if there are any elements that can be incorporated into your own stage directions. Is there a balcony? Can characters enter from the audience? (Make sure that they can get there from backstage, unless you want them waiting in the lobby until their entrance, which may be impractical.) If possible, make sure to rehearse in that space a few times to fix any technical issues and perhaps discover a few fun staging variations that will add pizzazz and dynamics to your own show.

The real spectacle is in the telling of the tale. Wooden swords are handy for characters that need them. Students should be warned at the outset that playing with swords outside of the scene is verboten. Letters, moneybags, and handkerchiefs should all have plentiful duplicates kept in a small prop box, as well as with a stage manager, because they tend to disappear in the hands of adolescents. After every rehearsal and performance, I recommend you personally sweep the rehearsal or performance area immediately for stray props. It is amazing what gets left behind.

Ultimately, the performances are about language and human drama, not set pieces, props, and special effects. Fake blood, glitter, glass, and liquids have no place on the stage; they are a recipe for disaster, or, at the very least, a big mess. On the other hand, the props that are employed can often be used effectively to convey character, as in Bardolph's aforementioned relationship with his wineskin.

PITFALLS AND SOLUTIONS

Putting on a play in a high school classroom is not easy. There are problems with enthusiasm, attitude, attention, and line memorization, to name a few. As anybody who has directed a play will tell you, it is always darkest before the dawn. My experience is that after one or two days of utter despair just before the play goes up, show day breaks and the play miraculously shines. To quote a recurring gag in one of my favorite movies, *Shakespeare in Love:* "It's a mystery."

ENTHUSIASM, FRUSTRATION, AND DISCIPLINE

Bring the enthusiasm yourself. Feed on the energy of the eager students, and others will pick up on that. Keep focused on the task at hand. Arrive prepared. Enthusiasm comes as you make headway. Ultimately, it helps to remind the students that a play is fun. I try to focus on the positive attributes of the students, rather than the ones that drive me crazy. This is easier said than done, but it is important. One season, I yelled at the group two days in a row. On day two of yelling, they tuned me out, and it took me a while to win them back. I learned my lesson; since then I've tried not to raise my voice out of anger or frustration. As I grow older and more mature, it is important for me to lead by example. It has been years since I yelled at a student group. If I am disappointed in their work or their behavior, I will express my disenchantment in words, speaking from the heart as somebody who cares about them and cares about our performance and our experience together. I find that fundamentally, young people want to please, to do well, and to be liked. If there is a serious discipline problem, I will hand it over to the regular classroom teacher, the administrator, or the parent.

LINE MEMORIZATION

Students may have a hard time memorizing lines. In these cases, see if you can pair them up with a "buddy" and existing friend who will run lines with them in person or over the phone after school. If students do not have such a "buddy," I volunteer to run lines with them myself. If serious line memorization problems arise that cannot be solved through work, then two students can switch parts if it is early enough in the rehearsal process. For doubled roles, the scene with fewer lines can go to the actor who is having memorization problems. Additionally, a few passages or lines can be cut. Again, it is important to address these issues early. Later cuts become more problematic as other actors have already memorized their cues. I have had to do late cuts about twice in thirteen years. While they have gotten us out of jams, it is best to assess early whether a student will have line memorization problems, and deal with the problem sooner rather than later.

In production, always keep several copies of the script backstage, as well as cheat sheets indicating cues, entrances, and scene changes. Make a prop list, indicating props for each scene, as well as props that are the responsibility of individual actors. Direct the Stage Manager and an Assistant Stage Manager to keep track of these items, and on show days, personally double-check if you can.

In thirteen years of preparing an inner-city public high school English class for a public performance on a field trip to the Folger Secondary School Shakespeare Festival, my groups and I have been beset by illness, emotional turmoil, discipline problems, stage fright, adolescent angst, midlife crises (not theirs), and all manner of other emergencies, including acts of God and nature. Despite the difficulties and challenges inherent in putting on a Shakespeare play with a group of young people, one amazing fact stands out in my experience. Here is how many times a student has been absent for show day: Zero. Somehow, everybody has always made it to the show, and the show has gone on. How can this be? It's a mystery.

✳ PERFORMANCE NOTES: *LOVE'S LABOR'S LOST*

I directed this thirty-minute version of *Love's Labor's Lost* in 2003 with a group of ninth graders. The young cast had a great time with the courtship, the mistaken identity, the silly Russian dances, and the play-within-a-play, "The Nine Worthies." The characters are colorful and the language is rich. The play is merry, but it also has a serious side, and it is one of the few Shakespearean comedies not to end in happy marriages. I like comedies that have a serious flip side, and young performers do, too. The contrast allows them to express range and dynamics.

These notes are the result of my own review of the performance video. They are not intended to be the "definitive" performance notes for all productions of *Love's Labor's Lost*. Your production will be unique to you and your cast. That is the magic of live theater. What is interesting about these notes is that many of the performance details I mention were not part of the original stage directions. They either emerged spontaneously on performance day or were developed by students in rehearsal after the stage directions had been written into the script.

Some of these pieces of stage business work like a charm. Others fall flat. Still others are unintentionally hilarious. My favorites are the ones that arise directly from the students themselves and demonstrate a union between actor and character, as if that individual has become a vehicle for the character he is playing. To witness a fifteen-year-old young man "become" The King of Navarre as Shakespeare's words leave his mouth is a memorable moment indeed.

SCENE 1 (ACT I, SCENE I)

This cast of ninth graders was responsive, committed, and enthusiastic, but they had one problematic quality that I failed to reign in by show day: they spoke too fast. Many young actors deliver their lines too quickly, which can confuse the audience. Finding beats and breathing points in the script helps control this tendency. Have the actors mark a slash in their texts at appropriate breathing points. They can also underline emphasized words or syllables, and experiment with changing the emphasis to hear how the line's meaning changes as well. Actors can practice "coloring" their words—think of the word as an emotion evoker instead of just a word. See if the word can become a poem in itself, with richness that echoes its sentiment, or enhances the image it arouses. This exercise will encourage performers to slow down their speech and allow the words to breathe and convey their fullest meaning.

Additionally, actors need to modulate their voices. It is helpful to compare the text to a song. Players can sing their lines to experiment with variations in pitch and tempo. They can also try saying their parts like a TV newscaster, an opera singer, or a grizzly bear. Animal imagery can be a good way to encourage actors to explore their characters' animal essences. Actors must practice *diction* exercises too, such as tongue twisters, and bouncing off consonants. Use these exercises in rehearsal to expand the performers' vocal range.

The interchange between Costard and the King in Scene One presents an interesting challenge. Actors should pick up very quickly on each other's cues, allowing the dialogue to bounce back and forth between them like a ping-pong game, but they must still speak at a moderate pace for the sake of comprehension. *Love's Labor's Lost* features many merry moments in which the focus shifts back and forth swiftly between players in snappy repartee. Precise blocking and timing are therefore essential to the success of the comedy.

Once the blocking is rehearsed and finalized, players can loosen up and have fun within the context of choreographed conversations.

In this sense the play is like a dance. In fact, enlisting the assistance of a dance instructor is always a good idea. Outside instructors in dance, music, voice, and other disciplines bring a fresh perspective and can provide exciting instruction and suggestions.

The original blocking as published in this cutting of the play has the King, then Costard, and then Dull following each other across the stage, each moving on his own line. As rehearsal progressed we found that the staging worked better with just Costard following tightly over the King's shoulder. You will find in rehearsal that this book's staging suggestions are a starting point for what will become the unique result of your own work with a specific cast.

The end of the scene works nicely if Berowne and Dull physically drag Costard away while he is delivering his "I suffer for the truth" speech. The action of really being pulled off the stage increases the urgency of the text, and forces the character to speak up and be heard amidst the commotion. (Maybe the next time I am having a hard time getting an actor to project, I will try having him recites his lines while being dragged slowly off the stage!)

SCENE 2 (ACT II, SCENE I)

Following Boyet's exit line, "Proud of employment, willingly I go," the Princess calls after him, "All pride is willing pride, and yours is so." She then takes a couple of swaggering steps, smiles, and wags her finger merrily in his direction as if to gently upbraid him for his pride. This garners a hearty laugh from the audience. The Princess physically illustrates her joy in a good jest, especially her own. This high-spirited gesture sets the tone for some of the good-natured pranks that ensue in this lively battle of the sexes.

The four ladies grin infectiously as they describe the qualities and charms of their respective love interests. One person having a lot of fun on stage is often all it takes to bring cast members and the audience along. If nobody is having fun, it is your job as director to get the ball rolling. Laughter and merriment are contagious. Bring your love of theatre and Shakespeare into the rehearsal process and joy will follow.

In our production, the student playing the Princess had an enthusiasm for her character that carried the other three actors along with her. The four ladies in this scene not only clearly advanced the plot, but also more importantly, furthered the fun.

The structure of the action and dialogue in *Love's Labor's Lost* allows for the technique of *freezing* the action so that the audience's eyes focus on one couple at a time. When Rosaline and Berowne are on the bench, all other actors freeze while facing in their direction, creating the impression that the wooers have stepped out of time into their own world. This is a great way to give complete focus over to one couple at a time.

As with the banter between the King and Costard in Scene One, the witticisms between Rosaline and Berowne bounce quickly here. The best way to tighten up quick exchanges of this kind is to practice picking up on each other's cues in rehearsal. Actors often memorize their lines, but forget to memorize the cues that come before them. Memorize cues too!

To enhance the verbal back and forth between Rosaline and Berowne, we designed physical moves to accompany the dialogue: As Berowne brought his arm around Rosaline, she stood up rapidly, causing Berowne to fall onto the bench. Berowne then stood quickly, and returned to Rosaline's side.

The words provoke a movement. That movement causes a physical response, which in turn elicits commentary, and so on. It is a dance. Rosaline turned her back to Berowne, who then turned his back and walked, defeated, back to his line of comrades stage right. He snapped his fingers, and the rest of the group unfroze.

There are opportunities for physical "codas" as the men exit the stage. Princess gives a little wave to the King. Berowne pauses and glances over his shoulder at Rosaline on the way out. Entrances and exits are often overlooked as opportunities to make a good first and last impression on the scene.

Boyet's speech about King Navarre's transparent affection for the Princess ends with the lovely line, "Methought all his senses were locked in his eye/ As jewels in crystal for some prince to buy." This passage offers an opportunity for the performer to enhance the flowery description through word coloring and gestures. Many of the words in this speech can be colored: "heart," "eye," "agate," "print," "proud," "form," "pride," "senses," "looked," "jewelry," "crystal," "prince." All these words can be enriched through vocal coloration. The actor simply makes a conscious choice to slow down and allow the richness and imagery of the words to emerge. There are some words (notably "heart" and "eye") which can be accompanied by simple gestures (placing the hand over the heart; pointing to the eye) which further enrich the speech.

SCENE 3 (ACT V, SCENE II)

I can't emphasize enough how important it is for actors to make their own choices to portray a character. Having said that, there is nothing wrong with suggesting a number of possibilities. Young actors need direction, but once they are in motion, their natural personality and talents emerge, and they bring their own magic to a scene.

The narrator in this scene has the line "How will it all end"? After delivering the question, she skipped offstage merrily. This was her choice, and I imagine she did it just for fun once in rehearsal, and I urged her to keep it. I would not want a narrator to skip off stage in King Lear. But this is *Love's Labor's Lost*. The actress successfully absorbed and reflected the lighthearted mood of the play.

The "Russians" enter this scene wearing Fez hats, dark goatees, and ridiculously glued-on black bushy false eyebrows: a nice touch! Gypsy dance music plays and the four performers commence a high-stepping, leg-kicking Cossack dance with tassels flying off their hats. The audience claps loudly in rhythm, and to end the dance, the Russians throw their arms upward in tight unison and let out an exuberant cry of "Woo!" The audience erupts in approving applause.

When there is a moment in a comedy where over-the-top silliness, music, dancing, and goofy costumes are called for, don't hold back. Insist that your thespians exaggerate the comedy past the point that they might be comfortable, and ask them to trust you, because it will pay off. It's worth a try! We employed the freezing technique again in this scene, in keeping with the notion that pieces of stage business are best repeated if possible, to develop a movement language for your production. The freezing was choreographed in a slightly different fashion in Scene Three. After each man wooed his respective woman, the couples froze two by two, until all actors were frozen for a brief moment. Then Rosaline and King unfroze, and when Rosaline said, "break off," all unfroze.

This production of Love's Labor's Lost closes with the comical play-within-a-play, "The Nine Worthies." This gives us another opportunity for silly costuming. Our 2003 performance featured plastic-horned, fur-trimmed Viking helmets, gaudily adorned plastic shields, and wooden swords. These are good outfits in which to strike exaggerated, silly poses.

When Pompey enters and exclaims, "and lay my arms before the legs of this sweet lass of France," he mistakenly kneels at Berowne's feet, and Berowne points across the stage toward the Princess, setting a jocular tone for the scene.

The actor playing Dumaine took great pleasure in calling Holofernes "Jude-ass" instead of "Judas," as a setup to the subsequent puns on the word "ass." Shakespeare's bawdy and risqué wordplay holds a special appeal for adolescents (as well as those of us who have chosen not to grow up). Do not shy away from exploiting these "naughty" double entendres. Students and audiences delight in them.

We finish "The Nine Worthies" with an effective tableau: Moth stands between Armado and Costard, keeping them apart with a sword in one hand and an axe in the other. This particular version of Love's Labor's Lost, with the aid of the freezing technique, makes excellent use of visual tableaux. Once we establish a theatrical vocabulary, we use repetition of staging methods to create a production that has visual and dramatic unity.

The merry revelry of "The Nine Worthies" comes to a crashing halt with the announcement of the death of Princess's father. At play's end, each couple rises from their seats in sequence to determine the future of their relationship, and each is told to wait a year and a day, leaving us with a lack of dramatic closure unusual for a Shakespearean comedy.

What better way to end *Love's Labor's Lost* than with the cast reciting The Winter Poem in unison, swaying gently as a group from side to side? A pair of onstage cast members should start the group recitation as other cast members come onstage so as to preempt premature audience applause. In the 2003 performance, the actors' voices rose buoyantly into the high registers on "to whoo!" and my spirit rose with them.

Armado announces to the audience, "You that way," and then gestures to himself and the cast, "We this way," and we all travel the way of joy, in the performance of a Shakespeare play. *Love's Labor's Lost* is a colorful and enchanting comedy. Using this book as a guideline, I hope that the experience of performing this show will bring delight and laughter to both actors and audiences alike.

✳ *LOVE'S LABOR'S LOST:* SET AND PROP LIST

SET PIECES:

    Table
    Two benches
    Throne

PROPS:

SCENE 1:

    Scroll and pen
    Letter for Dull

SCENE 2:

    Paper for Princess to give to King

SCENE 3:

    Jewels for Princess
    Letter and earrings for Rosaline
    Gloves and letter for Katharine
    Pearls and letter for Maria
    Masks or veils for Ladies
    Shields, helmets, swords, axes for The Worthies

Wed. Feb. 26, 2003

BENJAMIN BANNEKER ACADEMIC HIGH SCHOOL *presents*

Love's Labor's Lost

By William Shakespeare

Performed by the 4th period Ninth Grade English Class.

Instructor: Mr. David Ritzer | Guest Director: Mr. Nick Newlin

CAST OF CHARACTERS:

Scene 1:
The King of Navarre's Court
Narrator: Christina Carroll
King of Navarre: Ian Cooper
Berowne: Kahniley Sangare
Longaville: Langston Tingling-Clemmons
Dumaine: Gregory Miller
Costard: Darrel Philpott
Dull: Alexander D. Lewis

Scene 2:
The King of Navarre's Park
Narrator: Ashley Wilson
Boyet: Leandra Jones
Princess of France: Brittany Worthy
Maria: Bianca Rosenblatt
Katharine: Lea Ada Marshall
Rosaline: Brandi Bell
King: Ian Cooper
Longaville: Langston Tingling-Clemmons
Dumaine: Gregory Miller

Scene 3:
Before the Princess's Pavilion
Narrator: Candi Cofer
Boyet: Leandra Jones
Princess: Angel Lee
Katharine: Jasmine Garland
Maria: Bianca Rosenblatt
Rosaline: Adeola Little
Boy/Moth: Candi Cofer
Holofernes: Ashley Wilson
Nathaniel: Christina Carroll
Don Armado: Shante' Mixon
Marcade: Emmanuel Anamelechi
King: Ian Cooper
Longaville: Langston Tingling-Clemmons
Dumaine: Gregory Miller
Costard: Darrel Philpott

Stage Manager: Ashley Ray
Technical Director: Lauren Morgan
Costumes: Cierra Jones

"A jest's prosperity lies in the ear
Of him that hears it, never in the tongue
Of him that makes it."
Rosaline

ADDITIONAL RESOURCES

SHAKESPEARE

Shakespeare Set Free: Teaching Romeo and Juliet, Macbeth and a Midsummer Night's Dream
Peggy O'Brien, Ed., Teaching Shakespeare Institute
Washington Square Press
New York, 1993

Shakespeare Set Free: Teaching Hamlet and Henry IV, Part 1
Peggy O'Brien, Ed., Teaching Shakespeare Institute
Washington Square Press
New York, 1994

Shakespeare Set Free: Teaching Twelfth Night and Othello
Peggy O'Brien, Ed., Teaching Shakespeare Institute
Washington Square Press
New York, 1995

The *Shakespeare Set Free* series is an invaluable resource with lesson plans, activites, handouts, and excellent suggestions for rehearsing and performing Shakespeare plays in a classroom setting.

ShakesFear and How to Cure It!
Ralph Alan Cohen
Prestwick House, Inc.
Delaware, 2006

The Friendly Shakespeare: A Thoroughly Painless Guide to the Best of the Bard
Norrie Epstein
Penguin Books
New York, 1994

Brush Up Your Shakespeare!
Michael Macrone
Cader Books
New York, 1990

Shakespeare's Insults: Educating Your Wit
Wayne F. Hill and Cynthia J. Ottchen
Three Rivers Press
New York, 1991

Practical Approaches to Teaching Shakespeare
Peter Reynolds
Oxford University Press
New York, 1991

Scenes From Shakespeare:
A Workbook for Actors
Robin J. Holt
McFarland and Co.
London, 1988

101 Theatre Games for Drama
Teachers, Classroom Teachers
& Directors
Mila Johansen
Players Press Inc.
California, 1994

THEATER AND PERFORMANCE

Impro: Improvisation and the Theatre
Keith Johnstone
Routledge Books
London, 1982

A Dictionary of Theatre Anthropology:
The Secret Art of the Performer
Eugenio Barba and Nicola Savarese
Routledge
London, 1991

THEATER GAMES

Theatre Games for Young Performers
Maria C. Novelly
Meriwether Publishing
Colorado, 1990

Improvisation for the Theater
Viola Spolin
Northwestern University Press
Illinois, 1983

Theater Games for Rehearsal:
A Director's Handbook
Viola Spolin
Northwestern University Press
Illinois, 1985

PLAY DIRECTING

Theater and the Adolescent Actor:
Building a Successful School Program
Camille L. Poisson
Archon Books
Connecticut, 1994

Directing for the Theatre
W. David Sievers
Wm. C. Brown, Co.
Iowa, 1965

The Director's Vision: Play Direction
from Analysis to Production
Louis E. Catron
Mayfield Publishing Co.
California, 1989

INTERNET RESOURCES

http://www.folger.edu
The Folger Shakespeare Library's
website has lesson plans, primary
sources, study guides, images,
workshops, programs for teachers
and students, and much more. The
definitive Shakespeare website for
educators, historians and all lovers
of the Bard.

http://www.shakespeare.mit.edu.
The Complete Works of
William Shakespeare.
All complete scripts for *The
30-Minute Shakespeare* series were
originally downloaded from this site
before editing. Links to other internet
resources.

http://www.LoMonico.com/
Shakespeare-and-Media.htm
http://shakespeare-and-media
.wikispaces.com
Michael LoMonico is Senior
Consultant on National Education
for the Folger Shakespeare Library.
His *Seminar Shakespeare 2.0* offers a
wealth of information on how to use
exciting new approaches and online
resources for teaching Shakespeare.

http://www.freesound.org.
A collaborative database of sounds
and sound effects.

http://www.wordle.net.
A program for creating "word clouds"
from the text that you provide. The
clouds give greater prominence to
words that appear more frequently in
the source text.

http://www.opensourceshakespeare
.org.
This site has good searching capacity.

http://shakespeare.palomar.edu/
default.htm
Excellent links and searches

http://shakespeare.com/
Write like Shakespeare,
Poetry Machine, tag cloud

http://www.shakespeare-online.com/

http://www.bardweb.net/

http://www.rhymezone.com/
shakespeare/
Good searchable word and phrase
finder.
Or by lines:
http://www.rhymezone.com/
shakespeare/toplines/

http://shakespeare.mcgill.ca/
Shakespeare and Performance
research team

http://www.enotes.com/william-
shakespeare

Needless to say, the internet goes on and on with valuable Shakespeare resources.
The ones listed here are excellent starting points and will set you on your way in the
great adventure that is Shakespeare.

NICK NEWLIN has performed a comedy and variety act for international audiences for twenty-seven years. Since 1996, he has conducted an annual play directing residency affiliated with the Folger Shakespeare Library in Washington, D.C. Newlin received a BA with Honors from Harvard University in 1982 and an MA in Theater with an emphasis in Play Directing from the University of Maryland in 1996.

THE 30-MINUTE SHAKESPEARE

"Nick Newlin's 30-minute play cuttings are perfect for students who have no experience with Shakespeare. Each 30-minute mini-play is a play in itself with a beginning, middle, and end." —Michael Ellis-Tolaydo, Department of Theater, Film, and Media Studies, St Mary's College of Maryland